To Clayton "1983"
From
Bruce & P.J. Larson

People of the Bible

The Bible through stories and pictures

The Birth of Jesus

Copyright © in this format Belitha Press Ltd, 1982

Illustrations copyright © Gavin Rowe 1982

Art Director: Treld Bicknell

First published in the United States of America 1982
by Raintree Publishers, Inc.
205 West Highland Avenue, Milwaukee, Wisconsin 53203
in association with Belitha Press Ltd, London.

Conceived, designed and produced by Belitha Press Ltd,
40 Belitha Villas, London N1 1PD

Moody Press Edition 1983
ISBN: 0-8024-0393-X

First published in Australia in paperback 1982
by Princeton Books Pty Ltd, PO Box 24, Cheltenham, Victoria 3192
in association with Raintree Childrens Books
205 West Highland Avenue, Milwaukee, Wisconsin 53203

ISBN 0 909091 17 X (Australian)

Printed in Hong Kong
by South China Printing Co.

The Birth of Jesus

RETOLD BY ELLA K. LINDVALL
PICTURES BY GAVIN ROWE

MOODY PRESS
CHICAGO

A great king was coming. God had said so.
And God's people were waiting for Him.

One day, an angel appeared to Mary, a
Jewish girl, and said, "Mary! You are going to
have a baby son. He will be the great king.
You must name Him Jesus."

Mary was surprised. She said, "But I'm not
even married."

The angel replied, "Don't worry. Your baby
will be God's Son."

The angel also visited a carpenter named Joseph, who loved Mary very much. The angel said, "Mary is going to have a baby son. You must call His name Jesus. He will save His people from their sins."

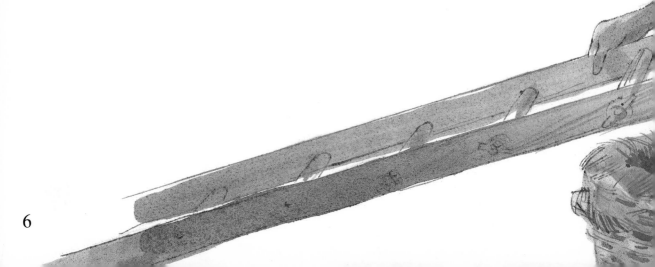

Joseph and Mary lived in Nazareth. Just before the baby was ready to be born, they had to go to Bethelem.

As they were coming into Bethlehem, Mary said to Joseph, "We must find somewhere to stay—the baby is going to be born very soon."

But every house was full. The inn, a place where travelers stayed, had no empty rooms. But the innkeeper was sorry for Mary. He said, "You can rest in the stable with the animals, if you like."

That night, Mary's baby was born in the stable. It was a boy, just as God's angel had said. Mary put Him to bed on the straw in the manger. She told Joseph, "We'll call Him Jesus."

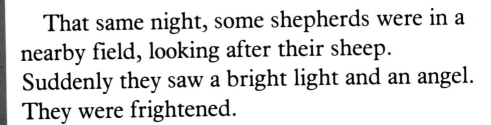

That same night, some shepherds were in a nearby field, looking after their sheep. Suddenly they saw a bright light and an angel. They were frightened.

But the angel said, "Don't be afraid. I bring good news. Today a Savior has been born in Bethlehem—Christ the Lord. He is a tiny baby, wrapped up and lying in a manger."

Then the shepherds saw many more angels. All the angels were saying, "Glory to God in the highest."

The shepherds hurried off to Bethlehem and found the stable. They went in and saw Mary and Joseph with Jesus. They were very excited and went away to tell everyone what had happened.

One night, far away in the East, some wise men saw a bright new star. "Look!" they said. "A special star! The great king of the Jews has been born at last."

A group of wise men (maybe three, maybe six, maybe more than that) made the long trip to the land of the Jews to find the king.

"Where is He?" they asked. "We have come to worship Him."

When King Herod heard there was another king, he was worried. He didn't want another king. He wanted to be king all by himself. So he said to the wise men, "Go and find this child, and then come back and tell me about Him." Herod really wanted to kill the baby king.

The wise men started off. And there was the bright star in front of them. It led them to Bethlehem. It seemed to shine just over the house where Mary and Joseph and Jesus were.

The wise men went into the house and saw Jesus. They knelt down and gave Him rich gifts—gold, frankincense, and myrrh.

That night God told the wise men in a dream not to tell Herod about the baby. So they went back to their homes a different way.

When the wise men did not come back, Herod was angry. He ordered his soldiers to kill every baby boy in Bethlehem. Would they kill Jesus?

No, for an angel had told Joseph, "Take
Mary and the baby and go to Egypt. There
you will be safe from Herod."

So Joseph and Mary, with Jesus, hurried off
in the dark and escaped from Herod's soldiers.
They stayed in Egypt until Herod was dead.

Then it was safe for them to go back to their hometown, Nazareth, where Joseph worked as a carpenter.

Jesus grew up in Nazareth. He helped His mother and Joseph. He played with His friends. He looked much like other boys.

But Jesus was God's Son. He would save His people from their sins. And someday He would be king. God had said so.

Moody Press, a ministry of the Moody Bible Institute, is designed for education, evangelization, and edification. If we may assist you in knowing more about Christ and the Christian life, please write us without obligation: Moody Press, c/o MLM, Chicago, Illinois 60610.

The Land of the Bible Today

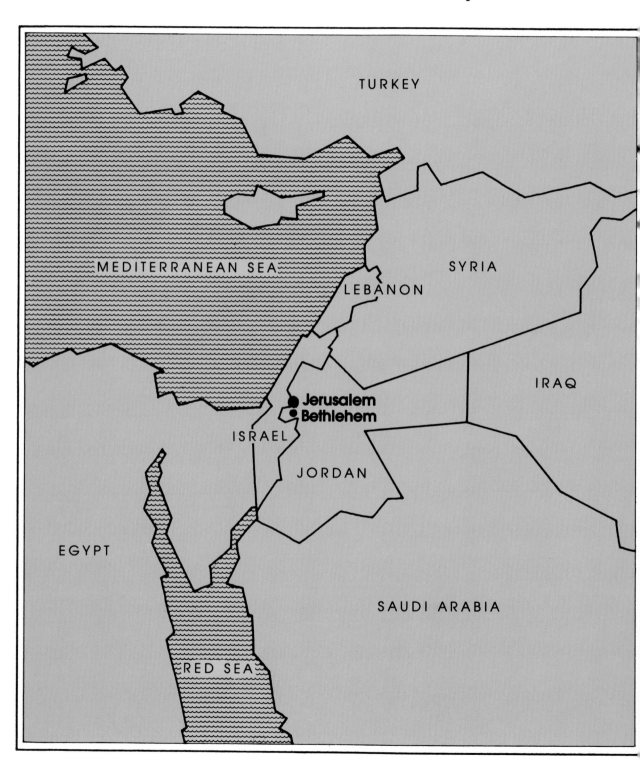